KOALA

The Story of Australia's Native Bear

(*Ronald K. Monro photo.*)

Surprised! Flashlight photograph, taken on Quail Island.

KOALA

The Story of Australia's Native Bear

By Charles Barrett, C.M.Z.S

1939

Registered at the General Post Office, Melbourne, for transmission through the post as a book

FIRST EDITION 1937

SECOND EDITION 1939

Wholly set up and printed in Australia by Brown, Prior, Anderson Pty. Ltd., Printcraft House, 430 Little Bourke St., Melbourne, C.1, 1939.

LIST OF ILLUSTRATIONS

———

ACKNOWLEDGMENTS

Thanks are due to The Herald Feature Service and The Sun News-Pictorial, for kind permission to use some of the photographs reproduced in this book; also to Mr. Ron. K. Monro, for a similar courtesy.

Above : Mother and Son. The beauty of Koala's fur at its best is shown in this picture.

Below : The Koala's Grip.

(Herald Feature Service photo.)

THE GOLDEN AGE—AND AFTER.

WHEN the settlement at Port Jackson was very young and strange new creatures were being discovered within cooee of the huts, a venturesome fellow reached the Blue Mountains. The story of his journey in January, 1798, remained unpublished for a century—and he remains anonymous. A young man who should be famous, for he was the first white to see a Koala, or at least to give an account of our lovable little fur-bearer. The aborigines called it *cullawine,* and the wondering explorer thought that it much resembled "the sloths in America."

Though the Lieutenant-Governor of New South Wales sent to England a description of the first specimens brought to him by the natives, the Koala had to wait until 1814 for a scientific name—*Phascolarctus,* meaning a pouched bear. Lieutenant-Colonel Paterson, a keen naturalist, regarded the new animal as a species of wombat, and the natives, he says, called it the Koala wombat. But in 1810 the earliest known figure of the native bear was published, in a very rare work, Perry's *Arcana,* with the title "Koala, or New Holland Sloth." There are quaint passages in the long account of the "sloth's" appearance and habits. The writer was blind to the charms of our "Teddy Bear," destined to become the most popular little animal in Australia—and the world. He uses such adjectives as uncouth, awkward, and unwieldy, and is "at a loss to imagine for what particular scale of usefulness or happiness such an animal could by the great Author of Nature possibly be destined." But the old wiseacre concludes: "As Nature, however, provides nothing in vain, we may suppose that even these torpid, senseless creatures are wisely intended to fill up one of the great links of the chain of animated nature, and to show forth the extensive variety of the created beings which God has, in His wisdom, constructed."

And now, with the Koala in danger of extinction, we look back to its Golden Age, and marvel that even the pioneers who saw it alive, failed to appreciate what every child loves in the form of a toy. We must remember that Perry knew the Koala only from caricatures—mounted specimens in a private museum—that of Mr. William Bullock, a goldsmith, of Liverpool. Doubtless they were "uncouth" looking objects. A quaint portrait of "Le Kaola" appears in Cuvier's *Règne Animal*, published 1817. But for the legend, one might be forgiven for mistaking this illustration as a rather poor presentation of a Manx cat, starting on a walkabout. It was not Cuvier, but a German naturalist who gave the Koala the specific name, *cinereus*, which is now always used.

A native bear climbing a tree forms the front page picture of *The Saturday Magazine* for December, 1836; it illustrates a general account of the "Animals called 'monkeys' in New South Wales," written by a surveyor who worked for Major Mitchell, the explorer, and knew his subject well. He had not only shot Koalas, but, with the help of aborigines, had also captured several both young and old, and kept them at the camp for some time. "Like many other animals of the colony," he writes, "they are drowsy and stupid by day, but become more animated at night, and when disturbed they make a melancholy cry, exciting pity. They feed upon the tops of trees, selecting blossoms and young shoots; and they are also said to eat some particular kinds of bark. When full-grown, they appear about the size of a small Chinese pig. They are certainly formed differently from every other species of the quadrumana, and it is probable they possess different enjoyments. They are very inoffensive and gentle in manners, if not irritated." Follows the description of how a blackfellow captured "a very large monkey in the

Albino Mother with normally coloured Cub.

act of ascending a tree;" how it was tied to the trunk of a
sapling with silk kerchiefs, but gained freedom while the
party was away. It was discovered "perched upon the
top of a high tree, quite at home," and recaptured. The
native climbed and slipped a noose over the victim's head.
After tugging and trouble, man and "monkey" reached
the ground. But Koala made another bid for liberty and
was knocked from the tree by a tomahawk, thrown by the
angry blackfellow.

This early episode in the history of man against Koala,
after the founding of Sydney, is not all savagery; for
Surveyor Govatt, touched by its pitiful cries, had the little
wounded creature killed to end its misery. And he tells
us that, when the native was trying to noose it, the "poor
animal, as he looked down upon his perplexing adversary,
looked truly piteous and ridiculous."

There *were* white men who could pity an inoffensive
creature in Australian wilds a century ago. Hundreds
who came after, were merciless killers—for gain or for
"sport." Millions of Koalas were shot and skinned when
their pelts began to be valued. Until modern times the
slaughter continued. Queensland had an open season for
native bears in 1927, when more than half a million were
killed. Do you wonder that naturalists fear for Koala the
fate of the Dodo? Another open season would mean
extinction, for since that year of ruthless slaughter, disease
has taken heavy toll of the survivors, and it still goes on.
It may be that Queensland's Koala population will vanish,
and the future of the species depend upon efforts being
made in Victoria, which has about one thousand healthy
"bears," jealously guarded. Long ago, they were exter-
minated in New South Wales and South Australia, though
in each of these States, a few Koalas are living in
sanctuary. Originally the native bear's range was from
North Queensland to South Australia. Literally in
millions they existed in Eastern Australia until the pelt-
hunters and disease, between them, had brought doom to
every province of their territory. Possibly disease, in

epidemic form, shares with shooters the blame for their disappearance from two States. But in the case of Victoria, it is more likely that "sportsmen" and fire brought the Koala within sight of extinction.

The young men and boys of an earlier generation, found it amusing to shoot native bears. Thirty or forty years ago, immense numbers were destroyed by these young vandals. Bush fires have done their share, and perhaps, as the Chief Inspector of Fisheries and Game (Mr. F. Lewis) believes, were, next to shooting, the most important factor in reducing the State's Koala population from millions to one thousand (the latest estimate.)

From a Golden Age, the Koala entered an Age of Decline and Fall; it has suffered, as the aborigines have suffered, from the coming of the white man to Australia. There is hope for both now that our eyes have been opened, and our sympathy fanned from a spark into flame. Humanity demands fair treatment for the blacks; and the whole world is our judge. The world too, is concerned for the future of Koala, because, through toys and pictures he is known and loved in nearly every country. Sentiment, if you please; but it has the right savour; and is not your love for your dog or your cat, nine parts sentiment?

We must save the Koala; not deserve the reproach of coming generations. Would you like to-day's children to know the native bear only as a glass-eyed mummy in a museum? Living Koala is a most delightful thing; dead, only pitiful. From this glance at his early lamentable history, we turn to pages much more cheerful.

FRIENDS IN FUR

KIM, the Indian boy, who lives in Kipling's greatest story, was "little friend of all the world," and that is just what our native bear has become, if only as a furry toy to millions of children oversea. Even Asia knows the charm of "Teddy," though what names they have for him in China and Japan I cannot tell you.

A duchess, fondling a mounted specimen at a bazaar in England, declared that it was the dream of her life to own a live Koala. The little Princesses, we know, would be enchanted to meet the Koalas of Phillip Island or the Sir Colin MacKenzie Reserve at Healesville. So would all the girls and boys of Britain. Once a sailor smuggled a young Koala out of Victoria and somehow kept it alive on the voyage to London; then he hurried across the border, for his home was in Scotland, bringing the most wonderful pet the bairns of the village had ever seen. Cockatoos and parrots were no novelty to those bare-legged youngsters; but a real live Teddy Bear! They gathered around it on the green. But the sailor, perhaps feeling compunction, took the little wonder back with him to London, and, the story goes, smuggled it on to his ship, bound for Australia. Perhaps, home among the gum trees, the only Koala that has twice crossed the ocean, told many times over the story of his voyage and adventures to all his friends and relations.

How can one help making them human, these solemn-faced innocent-eyed little fellows, whose ancestors were bigger than wombats and, likely enough, coarse-furred and ill-natured? You should know that fossil remains of the Koala and its relatives have been found, and one of these is named *Koalemus*, which means "a stupid fellow or booby." The fragment of a fibula, dug up in Queens-

11

land, enabled a scientist to recover *Koalemus* from the Past. He imagined it to have been a monster, an animal weighing about five hundredweight, or twenty-eight times as much as a living native bear. But actually our knowledge of the Koala's progenitors is very meagre. For thousands of years he has been the sole representative of the genus *Phascolarctus;* a unique arboreal marsupial, living upon leaves and as innocent as he looks, "a baby-faced bear," not remotely related to the Bruin family. Of course, he has a few minor faults, from our human point of view. He will use his sharp and stout claws if seized and frightened, and handling a scared or angry Koala is no joke unless your hands and arms are protected. But Koala never goes looking for trouble; he is naturally inoffensive, and tries to avoid even a skirmish when captured. Given half a chance he goes off on all fours in a hurry, making for the nearest tree. A mother "bear" with a cub on her back, wll travel in this manner, with surprising alacrity.

When a climber is still far below him, a Koala moves higher up until he may be clinging with those strong claws, to a swaying branch brushing the sky. He is quite at home among the tree-tops and should he fall —it very rarely happens—alights safely. I have seen a Koala shaken from a bough fifty feet above the ground, pick himself up and amble away quite briskly. But he does not like it, and is no rival of the tree-kangaroos, which leap to the ground as casually as we step from a lift. Koala makes forced landings. He clings tightly to lashing boughs in a storm, or sits wedged in the fork of a tree. He can go to sleep while "clawed" to the trunk of his home tree, though favoring a seat where a bough springs from the bole, making a comfortable V.

Disturbed from his sleep in the daytime, Koala looks down, with that wondering babyish expression that captivates everybody but the hardened pelt hunter and the "sportsman" whose creed is that all furred and feathered creatures were born only to be killed—provide targets for his gun.

An expression so mild and appealing, and quaint, a Teddy Bear's face, as you see it in some of our pictures, is that of a cherub in fur. An Englishman, Dr. Thomas Wood in his book *Cobbers,* has given the best account of the Koala that you will find in print—I mean of our Bush friend's ways and appearance, as observed by a nature lover. The most enchanting little animal in the world—that is Koala. But indeed there are so many passages in praise to be gleaned from literature that a Koala anthology would make a sizeable volume. This small book is the first biography which begins before History and leaves Koala as the friend of all the world, whose future we are striving to ensure.

We owe most of our knowledge of Koala's early history to Messrs. Tom Iredale and Gilbert Whitley, of the Australian Museum, Sydney, who discovered forgotten references in both scientific and popular literature, and unravelled the tangled skein of nomenclature. But they were unable to trace any very early records of the native bear's occurrence in Victoria, though it surely was well known to colonists by the middle of the nineteenth century. "The aboriginal language is dead," these two naturalists write, "the blackfellows have departed from the gum forests for ever, but still the little Koala persists, though in greatly diminished numbers, and long may it live to browse in peace upon the eucalyptus, if only to remind us of our heritage as Australians."

Our heritage! And we have been so careless of it that Koala has need now of all the guarding friendship being mobilised to save him. Governments and people must share the blame, if he vanishes completely: the former should have acted a generation ago; the people's duty was to urge and fight for protection from Queensland to Victoria.

Few Koalas have gone overseas; few, if any, are likely to go in the future. The embargo on exporting them is strictly enforced; though Zoological Gardens in the United States and Europe would give fancy prices for

native bears. We have none to spare. The first living
Koala to reach Europe became a tenant of Regent's Park
in 1880, having been purchased by the Zoological Society
of London. Receiving special care, it became acclim-
atised, and but for an accident might have survived for
years. Its end was tragic. On a walkabout one night,
Koala was caught in a washing-stand, and suffocated.

About forty years ago Koala skins were still reaching
London at the rate of 10,000 to 30,000 a year; and their
value ranged from fivepence to one shilling apiece. They
were used only in the making of articles for which cheap
and durable fur was required. "The Koala must be an
abundant animal," is Richard Lydekker's comment, in his
handbook to the Marsupials, where these figures are given.
In 1889, "the enormous total of 300,000 was reached." For
many years imports on a big scale continued. Millions of
lives were sacrificed for paltry gain. Fivepence for the
pelt of an animal which has no rivals for quaintness and
charm among all the mammals of the world!

The son of an English clergyman, who was educated
as a solicitor, and became a game shooter for the Melbourne market, has a place in the history of Koala. Horace
Wheelwright in his *Bush Wanderings of a Naturalist*,
gives one of the earliest accounts of the native bear in
Victoria. He wrote as "Old Bushman," and mentions
nearly two hundred species of birds and twenty-two
animals in a small blue-covered volume which has become
a classic of Australian natural history, though not
reprinted since the sixties and now a rare item. Field
sports were his recreation from boyhood, and coming to
Victoria in 1853, he earned his living by shooting after
failing to "strike it lucky" at the diggings. With a like-
minded man as mate, he camped and tramped down
Mordialloc way, and also shot game for the market around
Western Port—that is where he met with Koala.

This is the Old Bushman's description of the native
bear: "About the size of a large poodle dog, of a light
gray color, with white throat and rump, and no tail; and

a very comical-looking fellow he is, with his round bald face, small black eyes, and square fringed ears. The skin is very thick and tans to an excellent leather; the fur short and close. . . . I generally found them most common around about the end of autumn, and used chiefly to see them in the evening crawling about the top branches of the large gum trees, often with a young one perched upon the rump. . . . The bear must be considered as representing the monkey, of which animal we have none here."

What I like about Horace Wheelwright is that often the naturalist dominates the sportsman in him and, though killing to live, he could feel sympathy for wild life. Thus, he remarks that, because of their thick hide, Koalas are very difficult to kill. "It is cruelty to shoot at them with shot, if they are any height up a tree; but a bullet brings them down 'by the run'." The blacks regarded Koala flesh as a delicacy, and Wheelwright must have eaten it occasionally, for he likens it to that of the true bears which he had hunted in Northern Europe.

Fifty years after the "Old Bushman" had returned to England, Thomas Ward, a Queensland farmer, or grazier, was observing the ways of birds and animals. He wandered over the greater part of Australia, and from his journals and notes Paul Fountain made a book, *Rambles of an Australian Naturalist*. Several pages are devoted to Koala, which Ward met with on the slopes of Mount Kosciusko at altitudes of up to 2,000 feet, and also in forest country of the lowlands. He gives us glimpses of the blackfellows' methods of hunting Koalas and the cruelty in killing animals that are as tenacious of life as the sloths. The cubs were more esteemed as food than full-grown Koalas. A native, climbing the tree, would knock mother and young one together from the bough. And even a fall of 100 feet did not kill them outright; sometimes they were not even disabled. The black gins, with knives and hatchets, completed "the cruel tragedy."

Ward was one of the first to credit Koala with a certain amount of intelligence, though regarding him as a stupid

fellow generally: a view that is almost universal. Those
of us who have observed him closely, both in the wilds
and in captivity, are inclined to place Teddy Bear a
little above some of the other fur-bearers; for example,
he might pass an intelligence test too stiff for a wombat
or a ring-tailed opossum. But he certainly is not brainy.
The fact that Koalas once existed in millions is proof
that at least they were well adapted to their mode of
life; although indeed they had no enemies apart from the
blacks, unless eagle and powerful owl sometimes took a
cub from its mother's broad furry back.

Now that Koalas are threatened with extinction, their
export is forbidden, even to Zoological Gardens, and very
few are in captivity here. Koala Park, near Sydney, is
famous for its colony of native bears and Noel Burnet
has made excellent use of his opportunities to study their
moods and habits, their ailments, too. The thriving colony
at Healesville, in the care of Robert Eadie, as honorary
curator of the Sanctuary, perhaps is Victoria's chief hope
of saving the Koala for posterity. Many cubs have been
born, and the Koalas are healthy and contented in their
gum tree paddock. But a much larger area is needed to
ensure the future of the Badger Creek "bears." Other
colonies should be established on large and permanent
reserves, where the Koala's favorite food trees are plentiful. There is no good reason why the fate we fear should
overtake them, if the Koalas now living in Victoria are
provided with big reserves in suitable country.

A few private citizens are privileged to keep Koalas
on their estates. Sir James Barrett has four, which live in
gum trees in his garden at Toorak, and they are quite at
home. Thousands of visitors have admired them and
hundreds of cameras been clicked at these suburban native
bears. On his property at Frankston, Mr. K. M. Niall has
kept five Koalas for some years. They have choice of trees,
and may go for a walkabout whenever they please. It is
the only way with Koalas; to cage them is cruelty. If you
go to the Melbourne Zoo's Australian Fauna section, you

Showing His Chin-patch

Koalas often enjoy a Walkabout on the Ground.

will see a family of Koalas enjoying the open air life. Their enclosure is large enough, and they have an old tree or two for climbing and to perch in, as Teddy Bears should if they are to be happy.

A notable family, this at the Zoo; for one parent came from Queensland, and the other is a Victorian Koala. Their cub is the only interstate Koala in Victoria. There is but one species of *Phascolarctus*, though a North Queensland race is recognised, because of minor differences, such as shorter fur and smaller size, also coloration. If we allow that New South Wales still possesses a few wild "bears," then the present range of the Koala is from South Queensland to Southern Victoria. South Australia has long been excluded, but the discovery of a small colony of Koalas in that State was reported a while ago; may it be confirmed.

Efforts to establish the Koala in Lamington National Park, that wonderland of the Macpherson Ranges, South Queensland, are being made. When I visited Binna Burra, in the summer of 1936, native bears were seen in gum trees not a mile from the guest house, and one learned that they were doing very well. They are safe from even the pelt hunter there.

THROUGH KOALALAND

MY wanderings as a naturalist have taken me through many provinces of Koalaland, from the Tropics to "The Prom," Victoria's great National Park of 101,000 acres. Before the open season that was their Waterloo in Queensland, I camped among bear-trees at Rockhampton.

It was pleasant in the morning, while the billy boiled, to stroll by the riverside listening to bird songs and keeping a lookout for life in the trees. Many a sleepy old "bear" was discovered, up near the sky, and looking no bigger than a silver-grey opossum. Some were more than 150 feet from the ground. A young farmer of the district introduced me to his pets—nearly a dozen Koalas. They were friendly, but not over anxious to stay with a stranger. Their owner had their confidence, and affection. They climbed on to his shoulders, nestled under his arms, and plainly showed their pleasure. One sat in a chair when gently persuaded; another clung to a slender branch above. When their friend walked with me to the garden gate, he carried two Koalas. "They like to be with me," he said.

It seems so long ago, that excursion to Wilson's Promontory before we had begun to worry about the Koala. Though, around the camp fire, we heard tales of slaughter, the boundary fence was up now, "The Prom," a reserve and sanctuary for native fauna: the native bears were safe enough. Why worry? I doubt whether anyone gave their future serious thought, thirty odd years ago; certainly the Koala was not regarded as a vanishing species when I took the first photographs of wild life at home in Victoria's largest national park.

Under the Red Hill, I found them; scores of Koalas

The Prettiest Mother "Bear" and Her Baby.

Climbing a Tree in the Wild Zoo at Healesville.

in the trees around a swamp and trees growing amid granite boulders. This was their capital city—their head-quarters in a region long regarded as the home of the Koala. I saw "bears" in nearly every manna gum, a tree growing abundantly on the low hills of the Park and its sheltered flats. Often there were several in one tree and many mother-and-son snapshots could easily be taken. But this was my first experience of Koalas, and I paid for it when a young one was captured. The sturdy little creature showed its resentment by clawing a bare arm: the marks remained for weeks as a reminder that Teddy Bear has strong, sharp claws and mislikes being rudely handled. Of course the youngster which taught me this, had only been carried down for a close-up photograph, and was soon returned to his tree.

Huge boulders, fantastically weathered, are scattered among gum trees and Casuarinas on that hill overlooking the sea. The Red Hill some one named this windswept height, where thirty years ago Koalas lived in clover. Now you would be lucky to see one there. The colony increased until the food supply began to fail, and the Koalas at the northern end of the Park were threatened with famine. Many trees already were dead, as a result of repeated defoliation by the Koalas. This occurred in several localities, and action was taken to reduce the native bear population. Many, when transport was possible, were transferred to places in the Sanctuary where their food trees grow. But Koalas are not such stay-at-homes as they look; they wander far in quest of good eating; and when the stricken, but still living trees in their old haunts sprouted some foliage, the "stupid" little animals returned, to make them leafless again. That is the reason why now there are dead gums where once the Koalas had their capital. Many of the "bears" died, too, from starvation. Survivors wandered away to the interior of The Prom-ontory and settled among the blue gums on the heavily timbered ranges, where there are Koalas to this day.

Native bears may never again be as plentiful in the

Park as they were before the manna gums died; but are fairly numerous still on the northern and eastern coasts —the timbered areas, also among the big trees in the neighborhood of Sealer's Cove.

You may—most people do—believe that Phillip and French Islands have been haunts of the Koala for ages; but the white man is responsible for its presence on both isles, and from both it must eventually disappear, unless provision is made for a continuous supply of manna gum foliage. From French Island, where life had become too hard for them, because of their food trees dying, between two hundred and three hundred Koalas, some years ago, were transferred to Quail Island, in the northern portion of Western Port Bay. On this sanctuary of three thousand acres *Eucalyptus viminalis* grows in abundance and until the island was swept by bush fires the Koalas were holding their own. The colony suffered heavily in the big fires, and needed further contingents to populate even one hundred of the manna gums.

With the Chief Inspector of Fisheries and Game (Mr. F. Lewis), I visited Quail Island soon after its settlement by native bears. A memorable outing, if only because of mosquitoes, which don't worry the fur-bearers, but make life miserable for humans. It would be purgatory to stay on Quail Island for a week; we found a day sufficient. At every step mosquitoes rise in clouds, as one walks through the undergrowth, and by the waterside they attack in battalions. But the torment was worth enduring just to see Koalas happy in their new home. There were dozens of solitary old fellows and others about a year old; and many mothers each with a cub carried pick-a-back. By the way, often the baby, not long out of the pouch, clings to its mother in front and has protecting arms around it: is nursed almost in the same manner as you and I were nursed when we were babies. The cub usually is seen perched on the maternal back because it climbs there for safety when intruders approach, and also rides pick-a-back when mother herself is moving among the branches;

she would find it very awkward to climb about with the little one clasped in her arms; in fact, hardly possible.

A "great big baby" is young Koala, reluctant to leave his mother until he is about nine months old, though not wholly dependent upon her after coming out of the "nursery." When born, in the autumn, the cub is a tiny naked thing, not half an inch long, and grows so slowly that it is carried in the pouch for months—until September is nearly over, sometimes even until summer begins. It may be the end of the year before young Teddy feels that he has really grown up, yet he likes to have mother in sight even after declaring independence, and may stay in the old home-tree for a while.

Having ceased literally to be a burden upon its mother, the young Koala, sooner or later, may go wandering in quest of a tree of its own, or one already tenanted by creatures of his kind, but with room for one more. As a rule, he selects a comfortable low fork in a manna gum as sleeping quarters during the daytime. Being mainly nocturnal, the Koala usually sleeps or dozes away the hours between dawn and sunset, but often wakes up for a snack. When the supply of tender leaf shoots fails, a move is made to a neighboring tree.

Arboreal animals, Koalas look out of place upon the ground, but move along on all fours in a quaint lumbering manner. A mother with cub on her back was surprised at the base of a tree which she had just descended. Instead of climbing, she went off through the bracken in a hurry to a distant tree, the young one clinging tightly with sharp claws to her dense woolly fur: a rough ride, but little Koalas are used to tossing and swaying when travelling through the tree-tops with mother.

The native bear climbs ungracefully. Digging its claws into the bark of a tree-trunk, it makes a kind of jump, rests, then jumps again; a jerky ascent, but not so slow as you might imagine. Many a Koala has easily kept ahead of me in climbing, and I have seen a bear-catcher beaten time and again. Koala is not so stupid, after all.

When they were after "bears" on French Island—a round-up for the Healesville Sanctuary—often the hunt was exciting. Keeping to the larger branches until the man with a rope seemed likely to noose it, the Koala would suddenly checkmate by moving to the end of a slender bough which bent low beneath its weight. Too risky for the man to follow, and from his rope-noose foliage gave the animal protection.

Captives from distant parts of the island were liberated in a dead gum tree with lopped limbs, near the homestead, prior to being placed in box-cages for transport. One by one, they were clasped about the body in a huge pair of broad and blunt "nippers," and swung to the ground in a second. It did not hurt them, but, of course, they made a fuss: can you blame them? They were not to know that this strange experience was the prelude to pleasant life among manna gums in a wild Zoo among the hills—an ideal home for native bears.

An Interrupted Meal.

A Rest on the Way Up.

WHERE KOALAS LIVED ON WILSON'S PROMONTORY

MOODS AND TENSES

K OALA expresses his emotions noisily. In a rage, he grunts and grizzles hoarsely; hurt or frightened, he whimpers and cries out piteously, like a child in pain. Bear-shooters of the bad old days, must have been merciless, or else hardened their hearts against the sad appeal of a wounded Koala. We who think only of saving them now, wonder that men could find pleasure in killing these lovable animals. But—some men are beasts.

The hoarse, grating calls, heard often at night among the manna gums in Koalaland, are uttered by native bears; sounds almost as loud as those made by the big flying squirrel or phalanger, which break the silence of moonlit forests and startle a new chum unfamiliar with bush voices of the night.

Noise alone does not express Koala's feelings; his child-like face changes from innocent charm to misery as he cries. And when he is angry, the bland, wondering expression that captivates everybody, is replaced by an open-mouthed ugly look. Koala is at his best in repose; a perfect picture of innocence as, without a sign of fear, he gazes down from his tree, as if just a trifle surprised that you should disturb him. "The baby-faced bear," a small boy's description of Koala, is as good as a page of natural history on approved scientific lines. The fact that Koala is not a bear let the pedant mention as often as he pleases. Our "magpies" are not true magpies; the echidna is miscalled native "porcupine"; and there are many other popular names as inaccurate as "bear" is for the Koala.

Koalas are conservative in their choice of trees, being faddy about food. They eat the foliage of only a few species of *Eucalyptus*, their favorite in southern Victoria

23

being the manna gum (*Eucalyptus viminalis*). They are partial also to forest red gum (*E. rostrata*) and the swamp gum (*E. ovata*), the yellow box (*E. melliodora*), tallowwood (*E. microcorys*), and the spotted gum (*E. maculata*). An investigation of the Koala's food trees was made by Dr. C. S. Sutton, who contributed a paper to the Koala number of *The Victorian Naturalist*, in which he says:—

"Obviously the Koala confines itself to the trees mentioned because their foliage, which appears to be its sole food, is more to its taste than is that of any other species. Perhaps it is the manna in the leaves of *E. viminalis* which makes it preferred before all others. It may perhaps be concluded that the Koala does not object to a considerable amount of oil in the foliage on which it feeds, as that of *E. melliodora* has .866 per cent., that it prefers that which contains a good deal of both eucalyptus and pinene, and is not altogether averse to phellandrene, which exists to a slight amount, at least in some seasons and in some forms of *viminalis, rostrata* and *melliodora*."

The manna gum, a handsome tree up to 150 feet or more in height, ranges from southern Queensland and New South Wales through Victoria to South Australia; it also occurs in Tasmania where the native bear has never been found. In Victoria, this tree is widely distributed, more especially on the main divide where it grows at elevations of up to 3,000 feet; thence westward to the Otway Ranges. Another *viminalis* stronghold is in the south-western corner of the State. The river red gum, Australia's grand old tree, grows in all the States excepting only Tasmania. Yellow box, which sometimes attains a height of 200 feet (the red gum's limit), is native to the eastern States, but ranges no further north than the country just south of Brisbane.

A full length biography of the Koala could not be written without the co-operation of zoologist, field naturalist, botanist, and chemist, while geographer and geologist could each contribute valuable notes. The anatomist also must have an important share. Sir Colin MacKenzie dealt with the comparative anatomy of the Koala in his contribution to that notable issue of *The Victorian Naturalist*, which may be regarded as an introduction to any future monograph on the native bear. We quote the Director of the Australian Institute of Anatomy: "The Koala is an arboreal, leaf-eating marsupial: and in that sentence is the explanation of its anatomy. The lessons which may be learnt by the comparative anatomist from this unique little survivor from a past age are many, as will be seen by a study of its various systems in comparison with those of man." The Koala's very specialised diet necessitates vast quantities of tip-leaves to be ingested in order that it may receive its proper quota of carbo-hydrates, protein, and fat. "The response of the intestinal canal to such demands is shown in the six to eight feet long appendix (caecum) possessed by these small animals. The appendicular cycle reaches its fullest development in the Koala." In the case of the lungs, Sir Colin states, the Koala throws light on the developments of the human type.

You see, apart altogether from sentiment, our little friend, Koala, deserves his place in the sun—or rather, the gum trees. He is of special interest to science. But my own brief for him has nothing to do with science. I have been "instructed" by nature lovers to appear for the defence in the case, Koala v. Extinction. All nature writers in Australia, I imagine, are engaged in this case, and all are counsel for the defence.

The apathy of Governments is hard to understand. Had action been taken only thirty years ago, Koalas would have been abundant to-day in many parts of their range. An American naturalist, after seeing the lyre-bird and the Koala in their haunts, and hearing of the latter's plight, said: "You do not deserve to have wonder animals, if you fail to protect them against vandals, commercial interests, and the dangers due to settlement." In the United States there would be no need for public opinion to get busy;

the Koala would be regarded as a national possession and given the freedom of great reserves. I could only assure my American friend that the lyre-bird was safe, the platypus, too; while at last we had hopes of saving Koala.

There are questions to be answered—questions the reader is likely to ask, and one concerns water.

Does the Koala drink?—Not in a wild state; but in captivity it will drink both milk and tea, water too, and it laps like a dog.

Does a Koala mother ever have twins?—One cub is the rule, and the Koala breeds only once a year.

How long does the Koala live?—There are no records of longevity, but in sanctuary with abundance of the favorite food, Koalas might live for twenty years or more.

Are Koalas quarrelsome among themselves?—Yes; often two old "bears" will fall out and call one another ugly names, in their own hoarse language.

Are Koalas troubled by parasites?—Yes they are generally afflicted with intestinal parasites, and often suffer much from ticks. In Queensland, I found, lying on the ground, the bodies of several Koalas which evidently had been killed by ticks.

Are there any live Koalas outside Australia? — No; though many years ago some were taken oversea, and the tragic fate of one at the London Zoo has been related in an earlier page.

Does the Koala ever suffer from indigestion?—In captivity, unless provided with its proper natural food, a native bear very soon sickens and dies: chronic indigestion is responsible for this early death.

Young Koalas. The first photograph of the species to be taken in Wilson's Promontory National Park.

(San News-Pictorial photo.)

"Edward," the Little Orphan whose story is told in the text.

ABORIGINAL LEGENDARY TALES

IN many of the blackfellows' legendary stories Koala appears, and some are recorded in Brough Smyth's *Aborigines of Victoria,* two big volumes that were 'compiled from various sources for the Government of Victoria" and published in 1878.

This is the story-myth of Kur-bo-roo, as given by Brough Smyth:—

The native bear, Kur-bo-roo, is the sage counsellor of the aborigines in all their difficulties. When bent on a dangerous expedition, the men will seek help from this clumsy creature, but in what way his opinions are made known is nowhere recorded. He is revered, if not held sacred. The aborigines may eat him, but they may not skin him as they skin the kangaroo and the opossum.

A long time ago, Kur-bo-roo stole all the drinking vessels (*tarnuk*) belonging to the aborigines, and he drained the creeks, and made such a scarcity of water that all the women and young children cried aloud. The men, women, and children had no water to drink; Kur-bo-roo had taken it all. Much distressed and perplexed, the aborigines gave way at length to extreme despair, for no help came to them. Kur-ruk-ar-ook seeing all these things, came down from the sky, and enquired into the cause of this sorrow. Kur-ruk-ar-ook called all the bears to her and heard their complaints, and she heard also all the aborigines had to say, and she settled the quarrel thus: The blacks might eat the flesh of the bear, because it was good, but they might not skin it as they skinned common animals; and the bears were commanded not to steal the *tarnuk,* the *no-bean-tarno,* or the waters of the creeks; and all of them, black and bears, became friends by means of the counsel given by Kur-ruk-ar-ook. Thenceforth the bear became well disposed towards the blacks, and ever ready to give advice and help to them.

The superstition of the natives, in this matter of skinning a Koala was vouched for by William Thomas, whose manuscript notes are quoted in Brough Smyth's work. A member of the Yarra Yarra tribe when asked to skin a native bear which he had brought to the white man's camp refused to do so. But at length he was persuaded, by presents and an assurance that no harm could befall him, since the chief men of the tribe were absent. Thomas took the pelt to his tent, intending to make a fur cap; but the blackfellow became very worried. Remorse was felt for his act in skinning Kur-bo-roo. "Poor blacks lose all em water now," he said in much alarm. When his terror caused the "old doctors" of the tribe to ask questions, the culprit confessed. Then all was excitement. Thomas laughed at their fears, but was obliged to give them the Koala's skin, which, together with the victim's body, was buried "in the same manner in which a black man is buried."

There are several versions of the native bear story. One given by men of the Upper Yarra, relates that a piccaninny named Koob-borr lost his parents when he was about four years old, and the tribe he was left with treated him unkindly. When water was scarce he went thirsty. But one day, when all the people were away hunting, little Koob-borr drank his fill from the *tarnuks* which had not been placed out of reach. Koob-borr hung them on the boughs of a small tree, brought all the waters of the creek into them, then climbed up beside the *tarnuks*. The tree suddenly grew (like Jack's bean-stalk) until it was very large and tall. When the tribesmen returned and discovered Koob-borr away up in the great tree with their *tarnuks*, some of them tried to reach him; but he dropped water on to the climbers, who fell and were killed. Finally, by a ruse, he was captured and beaten until all his bones were soft. Then poor little Koob-borr was tossed to the ground, where

he was beaten again. He did not die, but changed into
a native bear, and ran up a tree. The big tree was cut
down, and all the water flowed into the creek; and ever
after there was plenty of water for the tribe. Koob-borr
became food for the blacks, but it was a law among them
that they must not break his bones when they killed him,
nor skin him before roasting. Should this law be broken,
then once more Koob-borr, the native bear, would become
powerful and dry up the waters of the creeks.

These legendary tales, "Just So Stories" of the
Aborigines, are entertaining and reveal the blackfellow
sometimes in a pleasant light. He had both imagina-
tion and humor; and among the lost tribes were old men
who could tell fairy tales in which all the people believed.
We should treasure all the tales that have been recorded,
though the white man perchance sometimes has added
and altered and misunderstood. I like to think that, in
the main, the legendary stories as we know them are
authentic. The tale of little Koob-borr might be told
as a bed-time story—it is more interesting than some that
our children hear on the air.

Clever writers, and some not so clever, have woven
stories around Koala, humanised our little friend of the
gum trees and brought him to town. He has been made
a comic character, with many adventures, and caricatured
in newspapers and magazines. He has been used in adver-
tising, and made fortunes for toy-makers in America; and
earned comfortable incomes for bear-makers in his
homeland. Koala has done more; he has brought tourists
to Australia and helped to put our country "on the map"
overseas.

Nowhere else in the world can you see a live Teddy
Bear—unique little Australian. His portrait, on a National
Travel poster, is one of the best advertisements for
Australia, so far as tourist traffic is concerned. Often
visitors from the United States, ask only to see a platypus
and a real Teddy Bear. Our cities mean nothing to them;

but they envy us a few of Nature's gifts to Australia, most of all the Koala.

There's a young Koala down at Cowes, Phillip Island, who found a human friend when abandoned by his mother as a baby. He was reared by Mrs. Oswin Roberts, to whom the Fisheries and Game Department gave a special permit to keep little "Edward" until this lucky native bear became old enough and able to look after himself. In a household he learned table manners: sometimes, as you see, feeding himself very prettily while seated on a cushion in a child's high chair.

Edward the Koala is a delightful little chap that any small girl, or boy, would love to have as a pet. But he is only growing up among humans, and will some day return to the gum trees where his own folks dwell. If Koalas at Cowes welcome him, we may fancy that it will be not as a prodigal but as an adventurous cub with stories to tell about the queer animal, man, a good-natured giant who for a century their enemy has become the champion of all native bears.

Edward's experience is unique, for a Koala. Many of his kind have been pampered; but not adopted as little brothers, with a seat at table and all that. His biography is "to be continued," and every prospect is pleasant for the tamest of all Teddy Bears. He is in no hurry to leave his friends, and indeed he could not be happier in a gum tree, or safer, than he is as a member of an island household.

Young Edward's ancestors came from the mainland. Thirty odd years ago some of the Corinella fishermen took a few Koalas to French Island, and from there they were introduced to Phillip Island. While the descendants of these pioneers are numerous, you might search the bush for miles around Corinella now without finding more than two or three native bears. There was one old fellow in a gum tree near the school when I last visited Corinella. Some of the children took me to meet him; they seemed to be rather proud of their tame-wild pet.

(*Sun News-Pictorial photo.*)

"Edward" at the Breakfast Table.

Koala with a Superior Air.

Round about Western Port Koalas live still, but they are scarce and scattered. Long ago, there were thousands of them, and Corinella had its share. That township with a musical name that chimes in with Koala, has a place in the history of Victoria: a very early attempt at settlement was made there, and the visitor sees relics and feels the touch of Romance on the shores of Western Port Bay. I like to think of Corinella, not only as a historic township, but also as a link with the past of Phillip Island's colony of Koalas. Did the first settlers there take toll or leave them in peace to munch gum leaves and look wonderingly down at the strange newcomers from the sea? Doubtless a few were shot, for sport or out of curiosity. But the founders of Corinella had their trials and tribulations, and one imagines, not very much leisure for holiday excursions with the gun. It happened so long ago, and we may never know even why gun-pits were dug in the cliff, or who gave the tiny settlement its name like a wild bird's song.

Brown, Prior, Anderson Pty. Ltd., 430 Little Bourke St., Melb., C.1.

www.ingramcontent.com/pod-product-compliance
Lightning Source LLC
Chambersburg PA
CBHW060650290526
45793CB00001B/484